Old Hessle

with Anlaby, North Ferriby, Swanland, West Ella and Willerby

Eastgate was the road which ran alongside the eastern extremity of Hessle and bordered Hessle Common. The suffix 'gate' is from the old Scandinavian word 'gata' meaning road, and does not necessarily denote the presence of a gate of any kind. York and Cottingham have similar examples of gateless gates. In Hessle there are several gates: Northgate, Eastgate, Southgate, Swinegate and Prestongate. The derivation of the first three is obvious: Northgate was the road which led north, to Beverley, and Southgate led south, to the ferry at the haven. These two formed part of what has been called the 'Pilgrims' Way'. This ancient highway followed the Roman road and used the Hessle–Barton ferry as the vital link in journeys between Lincoln and Durham and beyond, and was used by pilgrims travelling to the shrine of St. John of Beverley. The northern part of Southgate between Cow Lane and Swinegate is recorded as Town Street on *Iveson's Survey* of 1853.

Text © Paul Chrystal, 2019.
First published in the United Kingdom, 2019,
by Stenlake Publishing Ltd.
Telephone: 01290 551122
www.stenlake.co.uk

ISBN 9781840338386

The publishers regret that they cannot supply copies of any pictures featured in this book.

Also by Paul Chrystal for Stenlake Publishing:

Old Bournville
Durham's Days of Steam (with Stan Laundon)
Old Eston & Nomanby
Old Haxby & New Earswick
Old Middlesbrough
Old Port Sunlight
Old Redcar and Coatham
Old Saltaire & Shipley
York and its Railways 1839-1950

York's Churches and Places of Worship
The Place Names of Yorkshire
Wheels Around Yorkshire
Old Yorkshire Country Life
Yorkshire Murders, Manslaughter, Madness & Executions
Yorkshire's Days of Steam

Further Reading

Aldabella, P and R Barnard, *Hull and East Yorkshire Breweries*, East Yorkshire Local History Society, Beverley, 1997.

Allison, K J (ed), *A History of the East Riding of Yorkshire (Victorian County History), Vol. 1*, Oxford University Press, London, 1969.

Brookes, F W, *Domesday Book and the East Riding*, East Yorkshire Local History Society, Beverley, 1986.

Brown, H F & Reader, M C, *The Story of Methodism in Hessle, 1820–1977*.

Crowther, J, *Descriptions of East Yorkshire: De la Pryme to Head*, East Yorkshire Local History Society, Beverley, 1992.

D'Orley, A, *The Humber Ferries*, Knaresborough.

Elsom, K, *Memory Lane, The Hessle Collection*, Avenue Press, Hull.

Fitzgerald, W B, *Hessle: Its History, Curiosities and Antiquities*, Eastern Morning News, Hull, 1885.

Free, M G, *Hessle in the Nineteenth Century*, Hessle Local History Society, 1994.

Free, M G, *Hessle Foreshore and Its Communications*, Hessle Local History Society, 1994.

Free, M G, *Hessle at the Time of Domesday*, Hessle Local History Society, 1994.

Free, M G, *Hessle in 1834*, Hessle Local History Society, 2007.

Free, M G, *The Hessle–Barton Ferry*, Hessle Local History Society, 2002.

Gregory, R, *Hessle Whiting Mill*, 1984.

Gregory, R, *East Yorkshire Windmills*, 108-112, 1985.

Harvey, C, *Hessle*, Hessle Local History Society, 1994.

Los, P & A, *The Hull and Selby Railway 150 Years*, Hull, 1990.

MacMahon, K A, *Roads and Turnpike Trusts in East Yorkshire*, East Yorkshire Local History Society, Beverley, 1964.

MacMahon, K A, *The Beginnings of East Yorkshire Railways*, East Yorkshire Local History Society, Beverley, 1977.

Taylor, M, *Richard Dunston of Thorne & Hessle Yorkshire Shipbuilders*, Pen & Sword, Barnsley, 2009.

Travis-Cook, J, *Notes on Ancient Hessle*, Hull News, 1909.

Woodward, D, *Descriptions of East Yorkshire, Leland to Defoe*, East Yorkshire Local History Society, Beverley, 1985.

Introduction

Hessle was originally larger than Hull and more important. This ancient settlement, founded by Ella, son of King Ida, extends as far back as the 6th, or 7th, century. In Saxon times its name was Hoesellea and it enjoyed the status as the meeting place of the Hundred, where political and legal issues were thrashed out. Its situation, between the Wolds (Hesslewood) and the low-lying salt marshes along the Humber on either side of the Haven, had its downside in that it offered a perfect landing place for Angle, Saxon and Viking invaders. The Domesday Book reveals that the Hundred of Hessle had eighteen villagers and a priest, and raised 16.5 geld units in tax. Its value to its lord in 1066 was £5 falling to £3 in 1086. It supported nine plough lands and four men's plough teams. The lord in 1066 was Edeva (wife of Topi) replaced after the Conquest by Ralph of Mortimer.

The Hearth tax returns for 1673 show 71 taxable properties in Hessle and 27 uncharged. The town now had a population of about 430. By the time of the first census in 1801 Hessle was a bustling and popular place to live, offering the merchants and professionals of Hull an oasis of peace. They built their grand houses on land released through the Enclosure Act of 1796. The 1841 census reported Hessle's population as 1,388. The ordinary people of Hessle, of course, lived in their small houses such as can still be seen on Northgate. Hessle Town Hall was built in 1897 at the top of South Lane. Most commodities and provisions were bought and sold in Hessle, as anywhere else. Wives too were put up for sale: *The Hull Advertiser* of May 15th 1813 reports how Robert Brown of Hessle brought his wife in a halter and sold her to George Hardy of Hessle for one guinea. *The Hull Advertiser* was appalled, describing it as 'a disgusting scene' proposing that prosecutions would be an appropriate way of deterring the practice.

Commerce was helped by a ferry linking Hessle to Barton on the opposite bank. Gislebert de Tison Ralph also had a stake in Hessle and the ferry allowed him to cross to his holdings in Lincolnshire. From the Haven (or Fleet as it was originally known), the King's highway ran north to Beverley heading for the shrine of St. John and Durham, and, via the ferry, south to Lincoln and London. The Ferry Boat Inn was for centuries a place of shelter and sustenance for travellers and later for workers from the local industries.

The 19th century saw the population in Hessle increase dramatically, rising from close on 700 to over 3,000, this growth fuelled by people moving in from Hull and by much-improved local transport and communications: first there was the 1769 opening of the Beverley–Hessle turnpike road; then the Hull to Hessle Turnpike road opened in 1826 and then, crucially, the arrival of the Hull and Selby Railway in 1840.

Over time, industry grew up at Hessle Foreshore; nearby chalk quarries fed the whiting works; shipbuilding and the ferry to Barton all fuelled Hessle's economic development. Chalk was first recorded in 1321 as being worked on the foreshore at Hessle Cliffe. Chalk has been quarried at Hessle for hundreds of years and was used in the building of Anlaby Road in the early 14th century and for most of the roads in the area.

The black-tarred Whiting Mill (built 1812) replaced an earlier mill using horse power to turn the huge chalk-crushing stones. The six storey mill had five sails until they were removed in 1925 and the machinery converted to gas power. Other mills, for grinding corn, existed at Northgate and Hessle Road. Providence Mill was on Hessle Common. It was also used for the building of the Hull–Hessle turnpike road in 1826. Northgate Mill was an early modern brick built tower mill on a three acre site – one of the first of this design to be built in the area. In 1826 it was to let as: 'all that substantially brick wind corn mill built on the most approved principle, and turns, and clothes herself. Has four sails and contains two pairs of blue stones, and one pair of grey stones, with screens, flour machines and every other requisite article in good preservation. There are also extensive granaries, and a good dwelling house with sheds, cart houses, dove cot, pigeries, yard, and garden, and about three acres of good rich pasture land.'

In 1865 a chapel of ease and mission room, St. Mary's, was built at Hessle Cliffe to cater for the people living there as well as workers from the chalk quarries and whiting works. The chapel was directly to the east of the Whiting Mill. The single-storey brick building sported a bell on the roof at the rear and a cross to the front. It closed in the 1930s. Other places of worship included All Saints Anglican Church; St. James; Springville; and Our Lady of Lourdes Roman Catholic Church. The United Free Methodists built a chapel in Northgate in 1863 which later transformed into a club and was demolished in the 1970s. They used a larger chapel in Southgate, which had belonged to the Primitive Methodists for 52 years. There was a Primitive Methodist chapel in an upper room in Chapel Yard, Southgate. The Primitive Methodist then opened a chapel in Southgate in 1857 and worshipped there for 52 years before moving to South Lane in 1909. The population of Hessle at the time was around 1,500 and the new chapel seated 224 ("around 300 in an emergency"). The site was taken over by the United Methodists (formerly the United Free Methodists). In 1973 the Primitive Methodists united with the Hessle Wesleyan Methodists and the United Free Methodists to form Hessle Methodist Church, occupying premises on Tower Hill. Congregationalists arrived in Hessle in 1897 when they worshipped in a tin tabernacle in South Lane accommodating 200 worshippers. It was replaced in 1900 by the Trinity Congregational Chapel, later to become the United Reformed Church. This was closed in 1978 and demolished the following year. The Primitives first arrived in Hull, pioneered by a number of women, notably Jane Brown, who had been sent to mission to the area. She had preached at Hessle and in a building which had been a female penitentiary in Church Street, Wincolmlee, Hull. *Iveson's Survey* of 1853 records a Ranter's Chapel in Crosier Lane. William Clowes, one of the founders of the Primitives, preached in Hull in 1810 and was dubbed "Ranter Preacher".

Today Hessle is synonymous with the breathtakingly impressive Humber Bridge which links Hull with the south and the east. When it opened in 1981 it was the longest single span suspension bridge in the world. Beneath the north tower is the expansive Country Park, and, along the shore, the ruinous old Whiting Mill, the remains of the chalk quarries and what is left of the old shipbuilding yards. Plans for a bridge originate from the 1930s and were revived in 1955. The Humber Bridge Act passed in 1959 and work finally began on 27th July 1972. Head in the sand opponents of the bridge moaned that it would simply serve 'bread vans to nowhere'.

A view from below Humber Bridge towers taken from the north bank at Hessle, September 2008 by Uncool Eddie

That's the Humber Bridge above the Wintersgill Cottages. The cottage on the left was a public house and bears a plaque in the shape of a crown with the legend "Three Crowns Inn". The cottages, which probably date from the 17th century, survived a recent attempt to have them demolished and have been restored. The "Three Crowns Inn" name is taken from the coat of arms of Hull and, like the chapel, was built to serve the needs of the workers on the foreshore. One of the landlords was partial to a spot of 'free trade'. Allegedly he smuggled tobacco and concealed it in his vegetable plot only to be rumbled by the revenue men: he was discovered digging up the contraband when customs men made a return visit soon after leaving after a preliminary search. Another building near to the Whiting Mill was the house called the Cliffe and an earlier house called Cliff Villa or Hessle Cliff Villa (which may be the same as The Cliff), were both on Hessle Foreshore. Both houses seem to have had different names or spellings of their names according to who lived in them at any given time. The Cliffe was the home of George F. Holmes, a member of a leather tanning family from Hull. A man of many talents, he was also a sailor and an accomplished artist. The beautiful house, 85 feet from the river, was demolished to make way for the Humber Bridge. Coburg Villa and the Ferry Inn were nearby.

Hessle is famous for its chalk quarrying which goes back to before the 11th century. Initially, chalk was excavated on the foreshore where it was accessible; over the years the quarries gradually moved inland towards Hessleswood and beyond Ferriby Road. In the 1330s Hessle chalk provided foundations for the medieval defences of Hull. Records show that Hessle chalk was used to pave Anlaby Road in Hull in the early 14th century and for many other roads in the area including the Hull–Hessle turnpike road in 1826. Chalk from the railway cutting at Hessle was used as ballast when laying the tracks to Hull and Brough. By the 19th century chalk was being crushed to form whiting which was used primarily as a filler in putty and later for use in the rubber, paint and plastics industries. Initially this was a small-scale operation but between 1810 and 1815 a number of the independent quarry operators combined to build a wind-powered complex which included a windmill to crush the chalk and power the whiting works next door: the Whiting Mill. By the 1850s whiting production at Hessle was on an industrial scale as attested by the existence of a second, steam-driven whiting works located 100m to the north west of the windmill. The last load of chalk from Hessle to Earle's cement works in Wilmington left in July 1970.

The Humber Bridge Country Park opened in 1986, five years after the Humber Bridge was built. The site has a long history of chalk quarrying. Originally the chalk was extracted by hand then taken by horse and cart to the Whiting Mill. The objective of the park is to balance recreation with conserving wildlife. Twenty-two species of butterflies (for example the meadow brown, gatekeeper, comma or small copper) are recorded across the reserve and mature ash trees are nurtured for their insects and nesting birds. Other trees such as hawthorn, elder and crab apple provide berries for resident and migrating birds. The ponds provide a home for amphibians, including protected great crested newts. There are three trails: Meadow, Pond and Cliff.

All Saints Church goes back beyond Domesday and was actually the mother church of Holy Trinity in Hull until 1661. At the beginning of the 19th century the churchyard was home to three small cottages and a pinfold; the stocks were nearby. In 1802 the church was enlarged with a gallery to meet growing demand from a growing population. Pews and seats were allocated to specific houses in the town. In 1857 further work was carried out to remedy the walls of the church which were described as a 'patchwork of chalk, rubble and mud'. The church was enlarged substantially around this time increasing its capacity from 500 to 1,000 and in the 1870s five new stained glass windows were fitted. In 1892 a peal of six bells, made from the four old bells, was furnished. The cabs are waiting for the more prosperous members of the congregation. The house on the left was Hessle House, home to William Murray MD before it was knocked down in 1932 to accommodate the church hall.

The 1911 census revealed Hessle's population to be 3,918. In 1921 Hessle Square was laid down. Thomas Banks had been elected schoolmaster in 1876 and the school was eventually named after him, but it closed in 1906 and was demolished, along with other buildings such as, the Griffin Brewery and the almshouses, to make way for Hessle Square. Before the Square, it was largely a featureless warren of houses, gardens, shops and workshops, including Alfred Grantham's pork butchers. It was formed by flattening all of the buildings on the south side of Cow Lane and creating a new road from the east end of Prestongate to Hull Road – more of a triangle than a square. On the west side of The Square two public houses survive – The Marquis of Granby (behind the East Yorkshire Motor Company bus, every fifteen minutes to Hull) and The Admiral Hawke. Between them are a pair of old cottages dating from the late 18th century. The former studio of Donald Innes, famous photographer, is at the north-west corner. Before Innes it was Bowser Appleton's shop (a watchmaker, photographer and dealer in fancy goods) and the Hessle Gas Company Showrooms. The horse buses, then the motor buses, used to wait there. In the Second World War there were four air raid shelters in Hessle Square. The Luftwaffe only managed one direct hit on Hessle – on a house – and only one registered casualty – a woman died in an air raid shelter.

The Square, Hessle.

Twenty-nine years before the square was developed, *Bulmer's Directory* of 1892 gives us a picture of the types of businesses and professions at work in Hessle: it shows the rich diversity of life here. There were five brick and tile manufacturers; four butchers (including the oddly named Jabez Sharp, Cowgate); eight cowkeepers (including Henry Bullock, Hull Road and John Lickass, Tower Hill); eight famers; six grocers; four laundry proprietors; three surgeons; and four tailors. In addition there was John Stow, essence and mineral water manufacturer, Hull Road; Benjamin Rogers master mariner, Hull Road; Henry Pattinson Henry, consular secretary; John Peart, fellmonger, Hull Road; Charles John Hudson, chalk quarry owner, Southfield; F. Lonsdale, secretary Hessle Working Men's Institute and Reading Room, Southgate; M. Samuelson, managing director Hessle Gas, Light, & Coke Co., Ltd works, Waterside; David Hearfield, stone merchant, lime burner and whiting manufacturer, Hessle Common and Cliff works; James Curtis, head gamekeeper, Hesslewood; and George Bohn, architect, Tranby Park.

Southgate from the north looking towards the square. Boots is on the south side of the Square continuing the tradition of chemists and druggists on the site: formerly it was the premises of H E Brown, the chemist. He was re-located from the original corner of Cow Lane and insisted on having an open access to his shop with no urinals outside. This was also home to Hessle Fire Station and Griffin's garage (later Welpton's) with petrol pumps jutting from the wall with an overhead hose. At the end was Banks' school on the site of the school and hospital endowed by Leonard Chamberlain in 1716. This comprised three almshouses below and the school above. To the west was the Griffin Brewery. Bowser Appleton's, watchmakers, on the corner is at the top of Southgate, later to become premises for Donald Innes Photographic Studio.

Fitzgerald tells us in *Hessle; Its History, Curiosities and Antiquities* that Prestongate was originally called Westgate. It may have been changed because a family called Preston lived here and gave their name to the street. Preston is derived from Priest or Priestman and is one of our oldest surnames. Just as likely is that it derives from someone who came from a place called Preston. Prestongate was once the main turnpike road from Hessle to Ferriby and the main road from Hull to the west. The half-timbered house on the north west corner is 18th century and was once owned by the Spicer family. The Spicers were farmers, coal merchants, landlords and held the rights to the ferry to Barton. The site of the short-lived Hessle Market towards the end of the 20th century was here. Other Prestongate businesses included Leonard Wilson plumber and water engineer, saddlers William Everitt Tadman at no. 18 ('for repairs to portmanteau, dresses and baskets') and Richard Wood's hairdressers next door to him.

Jackson's of Hull, in Hessle. William Jackson opened his first shop at 28 Scale Lane, Hull in September 1851 on the afternoon of his wedding. Parsimony, or value for money, has been an abiding principle: the Jacksons were known locally as Mr & Mrs Split Currant. Under William's son, George, the firm moved to 127 Spring Bank. By 1912 there were seventeen shops, a bakery in Derringham Street, a jam factory, warehousing and stables. By 1916 there were thirteen stores rising to 85 in 1939. Today Wm Jackson Food Group owns a number of companies including Jackson's Bakery on the Derringham Street site. The Hessle Square branch opened in 1927; it is decked out for George VI's coronation in May 1937, with shop manager Mr Allington in the dark coat on the right.

Cow Lane, also known as Hull Road, many years before the Square was built in 1922. The Marquis of Granby or Granby Hotel, Southgate, run by E. Saunders, brewer, is in the background. The current pub replaced the original which was demolished in 1939. The Granby was named after the Marquess of Granby, John Manners (1721–1770), the eldest son of the 3rd Duke of Rutland. He was educated at Eton and Trinity College, Cambridge before becoming M P for Grantham in 1742, though his greatest fame was as a soldier. During the Jacobite Rebellion of 1745 Manners served on the staff of 'butcher' Duke of Cumberland. He served in Flanders in 1747 and in 1759 when his commander, Lord George Sackville, failed to lead the cavalry into action against the French at the battle of Minden Granby was incandescent. Sackville was relieved of his command and in 1760 Granby led the same cavalry regiment to a spectacular victory at Warburg. The Admiral Hawke was one of four pubs or inns in the town; the others were the Ferry Boat Inn in the Haven run by Thomas Kershaw, who was also a coal dealer – probably the oldest of Hessle's hostelries it also went by the names the Ship, the Sloop, The Ferry, Ferry Inn and the Ferry Boat; the George Inn, Prestongate was also known as the 'Top House'. Prestongate is home of the George pub. More recent Hessle pubs include the Norland on Hull Road, named after the North Sea Ferry that served as a troop ship in the Falklands War. It was originally called the Eight Bells. The Hase, opposite the church, took its name from the Domesday Book name for Hessle; it was formerly called Denton's. The Country Park Inn and Darley's, which takes its name from the brewers, Darley's, once of the Thorne brewery was built in the 1930s on Boothferry Road and after the Humber Bridge was opened was called the Humber Bridge: locals insisted on using the original name so this was resurrected by the brewery.

Like any other town, Hessle was well served by inns, pubs and brewhouses in the 19th and 20th centuries. The Granby was a coaching inn and a staging point on the road from Hull for coaches such as the 'Rapid' (to Manchester), the 'Royal Eclipse' (to Selby), the Royal Mail coach (to Doncaster) and the coach to South Cave, the 'Miles'. The Regatta, Ship and Sloop were all near the Haven. The Admiral Hawke stands on the corner of The Square and Prestongate. The name comes from a famous naval commander attaining the rank of Rear Admiral of the White in 1747 when his fleet defeated and captured much of a French squadron off Cape Finistere; in 1759 Hawke engaged the French Fleet in Quiberon Bay capturing five ships and running others aground. From 1766 to 1771 Hawke was First Lord of the Admiralty and in 1768 he was Admiral of the Fleet. The pub was auctioned in 1814 when its owner Robert Pinning retired; Pinning, who was also a partner in a chalk and Paris White business ran the Admiral Hawke for 30 years. There was also the Blue Plough in the 19th century. The Coburg was near the station. The Commercial Hotel stood on the west side of Hessle Square between the Marquis of Granby and the church. It was a temperance hotel. Despite the relocation of the ferry after the arrival of the railway, the Ferry Boat Inn continued to thrive. Directories record an inn around here as the Ship, the Sloop, The Ferry, Ferry Inn and the Ferry Boat – most probably all the same establishment. The George was in Prestongate, named after George IV. Before that it was called The White Gate until around 1860 with its sign a small white gate.

The British (or Parish School), Cow Lane (later Banks' School) and Griffin Brewery in Cow Lane. The school is in the foreground, opened in around 1661; Griffin Brewery is the building at the far end. In 1876 Thomas Banks was voted schoolmaster – the school was later named after him. It closed in 1906 and was demolished to make way for Hessle Square in 1921. A hospital and school were built here by the Rev. Joseph Wilson, and endowed by Leonard Chamberlain in 1716. On the ground floor were three rooms for three alms people, each of whom received £1 7s.6d. quarterly; and above it a schoolroom for 23 scholars: 'to teach and learn well to read English, twenty children of the poorest people in Hessle of what persuasion whatever'. Kingston College stood on the corner of Eastgate and Cow Lane and was run by the Reverend Voysey. It had moved here from Hull in the 1850s. The Griffin Brewery was owned by Joel Riplingham from 1804; his son, Robert (born 1806) eventually came on board. Joel and Robert were still brewing in 1834 but Robert left for a life in farming, possibly supplying the brewery with barley and malt. By 1846 the brewery had passed to James Hood, a Scot from Dumfries, who also owned a beer house and five inns in the district. He was still involved at the Griffin in 1872 but by 1879 his son had taken sole charge. The brewery had passed to Morley and Dewhirst by 1882 and remained under the control of the Dewhirsts until 1896 when it was sold off.

These huge crowds came out to honour PC George Thomas Nettleton who died 20th March 1905, aged 44, killed while attempting to stop a runaway horse and van, which ran over him. The funeral here is approaching the Square with Appleton's on the left and Brown's the chemist on the right.

The Weir lies between Tower Hill and the Ferriby Road; this attractive postcard view shows the Weir at the junction with Prestongate. A number of 19th century houses opposite Salisbury Street are listed – 16-22, 24 and 26. Some confusion exists over the exact derivation of the name: the Weir is recorded as Westgate in deeds dated September 1840 because it formed the western extreme of the inhabited area of the township. It was also shown as Wyre on maps; the name may also be derived from the weir that ran along the route of the street. On Iveson's survey of 1853 what we know as the Weir is marked as Tower Hill and what we call Tower Hill is named Wyre Lane. Perversely, another map dated the previous year shows the opposite. In 1916 Emily Melinda Newton's newspaper shop was here. White's and Taylors is on the corner with Prestongate to the right with the Marlborough Club and The Hull Savings Bank on the left of the street.

Swinegate is presumably so named because it was the location of a pig market or of a butchers' shambles. The Post Office is here: Post, Money Order, and Telegraph Office. George Mallinson, postmaster. Letters, via Hull, arrive at 7 a.m. and 5-30 p.m.; despatches at 9-40 a.m., 12-50 and 7-30 p.m. Other businesses in 1892 included: Appleton Bowser, watchmaker; Ebenezer Frost, bricklayer; Herbert Hatfield, cab owner; Robert Haselhurst, painter; Robert Ramsey, also a painter and Ringrose Cherry, a butcher.

Southgate was what might be called a middle class part of Hessle, as evidenced by some of the people who lived and worked there, for example: Surgeons: J.J. Fraser and James Molineaux; Tailors: William Barron and Gabriel Cook Willey; Teacher: Miss E. Rowson; Watchmaker: Appleton Bowser, the shop is on the right of the photograph; Herbert Jarvis, hairdresser and Richard Whitelam, draper. By 1906 a number of shops had been demolished to make way for the post office and the public library.

The aftermath of the fire at 74 Westbourne Avenue, better known as Herbert Hickson's the butchers, 1907. The Hessle Fire Brigade cart remains on the scene. They were captained by William Coulson and headquartered in South Lane until their move to the Square in the 1920s.

Built in Heads Lane Tranby House now forms part of Hessle High School and Sixth Form College. It was built in 1807 by a Hull merchant and shipping magnate. The house was inherited and occupied by successive generations of Barkworths until Algernon Henry Barkworth, who survived the sinking of the *RMS Titanic* in 1912. After Algernon Barkworth's death in 1945, his house was bequeathed to the local education authority to become a school, which it did in 1947 as Tranby High School. Algernon was booked into a first class cabin (A 23, Ticket Number 27042) paying £30 for the maiden voyage. The first news of his survival came in a cable from Reuters and a couple of days later (22nd April) Algernon confirmed his rescue to the *Hull Daily Mail*: "Please announce Algernon Barkworth, Hessle, arrived New York on *Carpathia*, ex *Titanic* sank. Jumped into sea, drop thirty feet. Just before she sank. Swam clear, and saw *Titanic* sink. Cold intense. Held onto overturned lifeboat for six hours. Picked up eventually by one of *Titanic*'s boats, Suffering from frost-bitten fingers." Algernon Barkworth died in January 1945 of toxæmia, and was buried at Kirk Ella church.

Edwardian Hessle on the road to North Ferriby, 1905.

Hessle Railway Station, looking west about 1905. It was opened in 1840 by the Hull and Selby Railway and is 4 ¾ miles west of Hull Paragon. Hessle has had the misfortune to witness two serious rail accidents. The first was on the evening of Sunday February 21st 1847 soon after the train left Paragon Station: it was made up of mail coaches, passenger coaches and fish wagons, heavily loaded to need two engines: the *Kingston* and the *Exley*. The train picked up speed and approached Hessle Station. About three-quarters of a mile outside Hessle the journey came to a tragic end when the train rounded a curve and came off the rails resulting in the deaths of two passengers, James Brown, 'Crier of Hessle', and a boot and shoe maker by trade; his body, along with the injured victims, was taken to the Coburg Hotel. The other fatality was George Waring, a blacksmith from Dewsbury, who died of his injuries the following day. The second was on April 28th 1868 when a passenger train collided with a goods train at Hessle. The official report reveals that the passenger train was a market train from Selby to Hull which had reached North Ferriby, from where it departed five minutes late. As the train was approaching the Hessle distant signal the driver saw that the signal was at danger. The driver put the engine into reverse and whistled for the guard's brakes to be applied. This was done immediately but despite the actions of the driver, the fireman and the guard the passenger train collided with the van of the goods train at a speed of between 6 and 12 miles per hour.

Looking east, the station master's house, signal box and down platform buildings can be seen along with the original Waterside Bridge carrying Ferry Road. 1832 saw the formation of the Hull and Selby Railway Company. The proposed line from Hull to York involved 38 road crossings; more than 15 ditches had to be bridged with bridges over the Ouse, the Derwent, the Market Weighton Canal and Hessle Harbour. Three road bridges were necessary in Hessle – Cliff Bridge taking Woodfield Lane over the line, Station Bridge carrying Pit Lane (Station Road today), and Waterside Bridge for Ferry Road. Major engineering was required at Hessle Cliff, where a cutting 38 feet deep had to be made, entailing the removal of 230,000 tons of chalk. This was used to build an embankment three-quarters of a mile long on the foreshore at St. Andrews and to build up the bank near Hesslewood Hall. The line was unique at the time in having the longest stretch of flat, straight line – 18 miles – in the UK. The line opened on 2nd July 1840 for passengers and parcels only – unusually no goods. The first timetable announced departures from Hull at 7 a.m. and 10 a.m. and at 3 p.m. and 7 p.m. In August that year, Sunday excursions were operated from Leeds to Hull. One of these trains had 40 carriages and 1,250 passengers, which was the largest number of passengers ever transported at that time. In 1844 the longest-ever train arrived in Hull, with 82 carriages and 3,200 passengers. Between 1st and 8th August 1844, 18,500 excursionists arrived in Hull, at 3s per head. These trains all passed through Hessle.

Hessle has been a shipbuilding centre from the 17th century. Before 1897, wooden boats were built here, but that year Henry Scarr moved down from Beverley, where he had previously been in partnership with his brother Joseph. Scarr proceeded to turn out iron and steel ships until 1932 when the yard was bought out by Richard Dunston. It became the largest shipyard in Hessle, building vessels such as *Loch Riddon*, a roll-on/roll-off ferry launched in 1986, and one of four built for Caledonian MacBrayne (CalMac) for work in the Hebrides. The Hessle yard continued to trade as Henry Scarr Ltd until 1961 but then it changed to Richard Dunston (Hessle) Ltd. The yard built a wide range of vessels from barges to tugs, to liquid petroleum tankers to schooners. The *SS Sir Winston Churchill* was built for the Sail Training Association in 1966. During the Second World War Dunstons won a government contract to produce TID tugs as deployed in the Normandy landings and in the Far East. One of the jobs carried out by the tugs was to tow the Mulberry Harbours into place on the beaches of Normandy. Some of the tugs were sent to the US Navy. During the war women were employed in the construction of ships at Hessle, among them some of the first women welders. Dunstons went into liquidation in 1987 and were bought by Damen Shipyards Group. Richard Dunston's ship repairs still operates further east along the Humber. The other early shipyard in Hessle was Livingstone & Cooper's which closed in 1928. In this picture of the Haven, Hessle is *The Somme*, a general cargo ship, built in 1950 by Richard Dunston and rebadged in 1967, eventually becoming the *St. Patrick* and then the *Antonello*. The Ferryboat Inn is on the far right.

The Haven about 1900. Other industries around the Haven included the Hessle Gas Light and Coke Company and a brick and tile works. The Three Crowns was the pub serving the Haven and is now incorporated into Wintersgill, a pair of cottages on Hessle Foreshore right in the shadow of the Humber Bridge, as shown on page 9, where a landlord was caught with smuggled contraband. In 1789 customs officers boarded a keel, from York, off Hessle where they discovered six casks of spirits and fourteen bales of tobacco hidden under a legitimate cargo of coal. In 1882 £3,000 worth of tobacco was found in a workman's hut on the Humber bank close to Hessle having been landed from an American ship. A Hull man was arrested and found to have a long record of smuggling throughout Yorkshire and Nottinghamshire. In 2000 smuggling was recorded when a vessel sailed into Hessle Haven with cigarettes concealed beneath a shipment of timber.

The Royal Navy at Hessle Shipyard during the Second World War. Men and a woman are putting a ship's side pocket into position looking aft on board a prefabricated ship at the shipyard of Henry Scarr Ltd, Hessle.

The Bahama (IMO 5033703) was built in 1957 by Richard Dunstan with a gross tonnage of 204; it was a standby safety vessel but is now decommissioned. The official definition of a standby safety vessel is 'a sea going vessel designed, organised, equipped and maintained in such a way that she can carry out rapid evacuation assistance in the event of an emergency'. They are also deployed to "protect" offshore installations from wandering vessels. It seems that at one stage it was repurposed as a trawler.

Anlaby is 1 ¼ miles north of Hessle. The Domesday Book has it as "Umlouebi" or "Unlouebi", a habitation within the manor of North Ferriby with 19 persons including a priest. The name derives from the Old Norse personal name Óláfr (or Unlaf, Anlaf) and 'by', meaning 'farmstead', so "Anlaf's village". By the beginning of the 13th century it was "Anlauebi". The early people of Anlaby were a riotous lot. In 1392 some inhabitants of Anlaby, Cottingham and 'Woolferton' rioted over the construction of canals supplying water from sources near their villages to Hull; about 1,000 people are said to have laid siege (unsuccessfully) to Hull, and some of the ringleaders were hanged at York. Disputes over Hull's freshwater supply continued until the 1410s, with the villages polluting it, and filling in the channels. In 1413 the Pope (antipope John XXIII) had to intervene by sending a warning letter urging the villages to desist, after which the disturbances stopped. Over time a moat here has yielded up French pottery, medieval tiles and a Constantine (a coin from the reign of King Constantine of Scotland in AD 920).

The bungalow tea gardens pictured here were built in 1920. To cater for the growing popularity of tea drinking, tea gardens were established from the 1730s as adjuncts of such pleasure gardens as Chelsea's Ranelagh, Marylebone, Covent, Cuper's and Vauxhall in London to allow people to stroll and take tea, the fashionable thing to do. The idea was based on the Dutch 'tavern garden teas'. Sometimes dancing was part of the programme – and so was born the tea dance; promenading, bowls, gambling, fireworks and concerts added to the entertainment. Tea gardens gave women one of the first opportunities to frequent mixed public gatherings without slur or criticism.

Nothing much happened here between the 1890s and the 1930s apart from a row of a terraced houses built along Wolfreton Lane north towards Wolfreton. Springhead Halt Railway Station on the Hull & Barnsley Railway opened in 1929 and closed 1955. Housing developments took off in the 1930s, and by the 1950s housing extended along the roads to Willerby and Kirk Ella. Temporary housing estates were built on the edges of the village during the Second World War: Lowfield Camp, and Tranby Crofts, an estate east of Tranby Croft. Lowfield Camp was used to house people from Hull displaced by the Hull Blitz, and later used as a transit camp for the British Army of the Rhine families.

Margaret, David and Anne Reynolds 'Dig For Victory' at Spring Gardens, Anlaby Common, c.1944. The 'Dig for Victory' campaign was set up during the Second World War by the British Ministry of Agriculture. Men and women across the country were urged to grow their own food in the face of severe rationing and to mitigate Britain's over-reliance on imports. In the 1930s 75% of pre-war Britain's food was imported by ship and the German U-boat blockade soon threatened the home front with starvation. According to War Cabinet's records, annual food imports had halved to 14.65 million tonnes by 1941. The campaign's tagline "Spades not ships!" encouraged citizens to get digging and planting on all available land. By 1942 half the civilian population formed the nation's "Garden Front", and 10,000 square miles of land had been "brought under the plough". School playing fields, public and household gardens and factory courtyards were all transformed into allotments – even the lawns outside the Tower of London were turned into vegetable patches. Any waste food was collected by the pigswill trucks. According to the Royal Horticultural Society there were nearly 1.4 million allotments in Britain by the end of the war, which produced 1.3m tonnes of produce. Around 6,000 pigs were kept in gardens and back yards by 1945. Along with state investment in failing farms, the campaign led to the UK halving its dependence on food imports. *Photo reproduced by permission from Anne Ketchell (née Reynolds).*

The Spring Head Inn, in Wolfreton Road, Anlaby, was one of many Hull Brewery houses in the area. Hull Brewery went the way of many other independents when in 1971 it was taken over by Northern Foods and then bought by Mansfield Brewery in 1985. Before that, however, in 1782, Thomas Ward and John Firbank built a brewery at the corner of Posterngate and Dagger Lane in Hull. Ann and Mary, Ward's granddaughters, inherited the brewery: Mary married a shipbuilder, Robert Gleadow, in 1796, and their son, Robert Ward Gleadow, continued with the brewing business. In 1846 Gleadow went into partnership with another brewer, William Thomas Dibb, to form Gleadow, Dibb and Co. Gleadow died in 1857 and was succeeded by his son, Henry Cooper Gleadow. William Thomas Dibb died in 1886 on a fateful train journey between Bridlington and Hull; he had run to catch a train at Bridlington, making the guard stop the train so that he could get on. By the time the train arrived in Driffield he was found dead, still sitting upright in his seat. 1887 saw Gleadow, Dibb and Co. Ltd. wound up, and The Hull Brewery Company Limited was born. Hull Brewery expanded its Sylvester Street brewery, acquiring other brewers and bottlers, and purchasing licensed houses: by 1890 they owned 160 licensed houses. In 1925 it acquired the Lincolnshire brewery Sutton, Bean and Company with beer shipped across the Humber by barge. The brewery survived the Hull blitz, because the Luftwaffe pilots felt the need to use its chimneys as a landmark. 1949 was a significant year: it was then that the company launched "Anchor Export", a strong beer which kept and travelled well so that it could be taken aboard ships for refreshment on long voyages. In 1960 the brewery owned 206 pubs and 39 off-licences in Hull alone. In 1971 Northern Foods took on 212 tied houses and changed the name to North Country Breweries Ltd in 1974. Sadly, Mansfield Brewery called time on brewing at Sylvester Street in 1985.

Picturesque Welton is famous for the beautiful Georgian Raikes Mausoleum, built by Quaker Robert Raikes (1765-1837), in Welton Dale; he was a Hull banker who lived in Welton House. In 1960 the vault under the mausoleum was broken into. A skull was stolen, later recovered. The first recorded accidental fatal shooting in England was recorded at Welton in 1519. BBC News 14th June 2011 reported that the first time a coroners' court came up against the new-fangled problem of a fatal shooting accident was 1519, when a woman in Welton near Hull was accidentally killed by a handgun. Redcliff, in the east of the parish, on the Humber bank at the boundary with North Ferriby is evidenced to have been a trading site during the period of the Roman Conquest of Britain from the 1st to the 5th centuries AD. There was a Roman villa at Welton Wold, thought to be the earliest example in the East Riding; it was demolished by 340 AD, and the entire location totally destroyed by quarrying in the 20th century.

Brough was Roman Petuaria and the capital of the Celtic tribe the Parisi. Petuaria was at the southern end of the Roman road known as Cade's Road which ran north to Pons Aelius (Newcastle upon Tyne). Brough was created a town by the Archbishop of York in 1239 and is famous for its association with Dick Turpin. In June 1737 he stayed at its Ferry Inn, under the alias of John Palmer; he travelled to and from and lived in Brough until his capture and execution for horse theft in 1739. For many years the village was home to BAE Systems which manufactured the Hawk Advanced Jet Trainer aircraft here at Brough Aerodrome. BAE was formerly the Blackburn Aircraft Company and then Hawker Siddeley Aviation.

North Ferriby is famous for two things: its ancient boats and its 12th century priory. The village is the site of the earliest sewn plank boats known outside Egypt. In 1931, wooden planks belonging to a boat were discovered by the Wright brothers; two more boats have since been discovered. Radiocarbon dating puts the origin of the boats to the Bronze Age, between 2030 and 1680 BC, about the same time as Stonehenge was built. Bronze Age round barrows were found near North Ferriby by archaeologists excavating the land on which the A63 junction was built and there is also evidence of Iron Age and early Romano-British activity in that area. The first wave of Danes arrived here around 900 AD and set up a series of villages including what is now North Ferriby – from the Danish 'ferja' bi, place by a ferry, linked by ferry to South Ferriby. Ferriby Priory was built around 1160, of the order of Knights Templar.

High Street, North Ferriby.

West Ella is about 1 km west of the historic village of Kirk Ella. In the 19th century it was gentrified by the owners of the village, the Sykes family, and is now a conservation area. The name is Old English and means "Aelf(a)'s Western Woodland Clearing". There is evidence of human activity in the area from the Mesolithic period, and later during the Iron Age and Roman Britain ages. West Ella did not see the influx of Hull merchants experienced by Kirk Ella. In 1801 the village's population was 79; in 1851 1,851. The only large house in the village was, and is West Ella Hall, built c.1740 which became the property of Joseph Sykes of the Sykes family of Sledmere in 1756. The name "Kirk Ella" derives from the Old English, and meana "Aelf(a)'s Woodland Clearing with a Church". Kirk Ella features in Domesday survey as Aluengi (Ella); there is evidence for human activity in the Bronze age – bronze axes have been discovered in the area, Roman pottery period has also been found. The 1750s onwards saw many wealthy merchants and shipowners from Hull moving in, mostly westwards towards the higher ground of the Wolds foothills and in an opposite direction to the prevailing winds, which carried the factory smells and other Hull pollution eastward. The road from Hull to Anlaby and Kirk Ella was turnpiked in 1745.

An unusual cottage in West Ella. The blue plaque there now declares: 'Kirk Ella and West Ella FEUDAL VILLAGE (1086) Rebuilt in Gothic Style by Richard Sykes (early 1800s).' The stone lintel bears the date 1901.

To the east of Swanland are West Ella, Willerby and Anlaby; to the south-east Hessle and to the south-west North Ferriby. Swanland boasts two churches: St. Barnabas is the Church of England Parish Church originally from 1899 rebuilt 1992; and Christ Church, also known as 'The Church by the Pond', is a Methodist-United Reformed Church. Swanland is an old hill village on the edge of the Yorkshire Wolds. It is probably the only community called Swanland in the world although there is a Swan Land District in Western Australia. Not surprisingly there is a Cygnet Gardens in Swanland. The village name may derive from the presence of swans on the pond although sources are suspiciously silent on the matter. The Old Café on West End opposite the pond was added to the rear of the shop here in 1919 although in the 19th century it was a public house first known as the Fleece, then from 1855 to 1879, as The White Horse. In 1879 a man died on the premises on Christmas Day from consuming far too much whisky. The licence was revoked leaving the village without a pub for the next 100 years. Today the pub is The Swan & Cygnet.

In 1844 the population of Willerby was 214 in 45 houses. In 1850 Willerby had a Primitive Methodist chapel, a hall, Oak Hill House, dating from the late 17th or early 18th century, now known as Willerby Hall, and another large dwelling, the Summer House, later known as The Beeches dating to the 18th century. A mental asylum, Hull Borough Lunatic Asylum, later known as De La Pole Hospital, and a chapel, were constructed beyond the village to the north in the 1880s. Willerby and Kirk Ella Railway Station opened in 1885 as part of the Hull and Barnsley Railway which passed the main village close by to the south.

The *Lincoln Castle* at New Holland Pier in 1975; that's Yorkshire on the horizon. *PS Lincoln Castle* was launched on 27th April 1940, by A. & J. Inglis of Pointhouse, Glasgow and was named after the Norman castle at Lincoln. She was delivered to the LNER at Grimsby's Royal Dock on 4th July 1941 to complement the 1934 *Wingfield Castle* and *Tattershall Castle* built by Gray's of Hartlepool. She entered service on 4th August 1941 on the New Holland to Hull public service. The route was operated by the LNER until nationalisation in 1948, when it was taken over by British Railways until 1978, under Sealink management. At the time of her withdrawal after a failed boiler inspection she was the last coal-fired paddle steamer providing a daily scheduled service in the United Kingdom. Later, she served as a pub at Hessle, and then as a restaurant at Alexandra Dock, Grimsby. On 31st March 2011, the Lincoln Castle Preservation Society was reported to have purchased the broken up parts of the ship for restoration.

The *Lincoln Castle* at Grimsby's Alexander Dock in 1976 even though she had been shorn of her main mast and her foremast had been shortened. *Photo by E Asterion*.

The paddle steamer *PS Lincoln Castle* on Hessle foreshore serving as a pub; she was a ferry boat from 1941 to 1978 on the New Holland to Hull public service and the last coal-fired paddle steamer still in regular services in the UK. She was later moved to Grimsby and scrapped in 2010.